MINECRAFT SECRETS & CHEATS

2017

CONTENTS

10
GET STARTED IN MINECRAFT
The things you need to know to get up and running in the best computer game on the planet!

WHO'S WHO IN MINECRAFT
Get to know Steve, Alex, lots of mobs – and the deadly creepers!
6

14
AMAZING MINECRAFT BUILDS!
We've scoured the world to find some of the most brilliant Minecraft builds! Reckon you can match any of these?

101 WAYS TO BE A MINECRAFT EXPERT
We've got loads of top secret tips to help you became an even better Minecraft player!
22

58
ARE YOU A MINECRAFT MASTER?
Take our quiz and find out if you're a crafting expert!

Which of these blocks won't you find in Minecraft?

a) End stone bricks
b) Sponge
c) Primsmarine pillar
d) Stone

4

30
KNOW YOUR BIOMES
Cant tell from your jungles to your forests? Find out all you need to know about Biomes!

42
HAVE YOU FOUND THESE IN MINECRAFT?
Some things are easier to find than others in Minecraft – how many of these have you found so far?!

THE BEST RECIPES!
Need some ideas for things to craft and make in Minecraft?

ALSO...

PUZZLES!

BEST YOUTUBERS!

34
SHOWING OFF YOUR LOOT!

MINECRAFT JOKES!

63
PUZZLE AND QUIZ ANSWERS

WHO'S WHO IN MINECRAFT!

Minecraft is full of characters and mobs to meet. But how can you be sure who (or what!) you're seeing? With our handy who's who, you'll never wonder again!

STEVE: Friendly? Yes
Steve is one of the two default skins that human players of Minecraft can use. He's not called Steve in the game, but that's the name that Minecraft creator Notch suggested as a joke – and it's stuck!

ALEX: Friendly? Yes
Alex is the other default skin that human players get assigned by default when they start a game of Minecraft. She was added to the game for the first time back in 2014, and has been busy adventuring and exploring ever since!

If you hear a hissing sound behind you, run!

CREEPER: Friendly? No!
If you hear a hissing sound behind you while playing Minecraft, run! There's a creeper behind you, and it's about to explode! Perhaps the most famous of all the hostile mobs in the game, creepers are most definitely not your friend!

Mooshrooms spawn in the mushroom island biome

ENDERMAN: Friendly? Neutral

You'll find endermen in the Overworld or the End, and generally, they'll leave you alone. But if you attack them, or look at them from up to 64 blocks away, they'll attack!

MOOSHROOM: Friendly? Fairly

We love mooshrooms! They're a strange mix of cows and mushrooms, and you'll only find them in the mushroom island biome. They're certainly easy to spot!

ZOMBIE PIGMAN: Friendly?

Neutral Mainly found in the Nether, but a pig hit by lightning will cause them to spawn. They're slow, can resist fire and lava damage, and leave you alone unless you attack them!

THE WITHER: Friendly? No!

One of the two boss mobs, the wither isn't as tough as the ender dragon, but puts up a strong fight! You have to summon the wither to appear; when it does, it will attack!

Cave spiders only spawn in abandoned mineshafts

ZOMBIE: Friendly? No

Quite easy to beat, but can make your life hard! They'll attack you, and villagers, and call more zombies to help! If they attack villagers, they may turn them into zombie villagers!

SPIDER/CAVE SPIDER:

Friendly? Mostly not Both types of spider are neutral, but turn hostile in darkness! Black spiders spawn almost anywhere, while cave spiders only spawn in abandoned mineshafts.

SQUID: Friendly? They don't notice you!
Squids are neutral mobs that spawn in large bodies of water. You can kill them for experience and to collect ink sacs, but mostly they don't do anything.

ENDER DRAGON: Friendly? No!

The game's big boss lives in the End and doesn't take any prisoners. If you manage to kill it, you'll gain access to the rest of the End's mysterious islands.

IRON GOLEM: Friendly? Mostly!

You can summon iron golems to help you, but large villages also have their own to protect them if they get attacked. They hand out flowers to villagers and help you in a fight.

HORSE: Friendly? Yep

Horses (including donkeys and mules) can be tamed and ridden. Horses are strong and fast, and donkeys can carry chests full of items. A mule is slightly weaker but can carry a chest.

Villagers can be approached for trading items

ENDERMITE: Friendly? Nope
Endermites are the smallest hostile mob, and have a one in 20 chance of spawning when you throw an ender pearl. They attack the player within 16 blocks but vanish after two minutes.

VILLAGER: Friendly? Yes unless zombified

Villagers live in villages and can be approached for trading items. If you attack their fellow villagers, they get angry and may withhold trades, but won't attack you.

WOLF: Friendly? Sometimes

Wolves roam in packs and ignore the player to hunt down other animals, unless you attack one. Feed them skeleton bones to tame them, and they'll attack hostile mobs for you!

WITCH: Friendly? Never

Witches live in witch huts and spawn at night. If a villager gets hit by lightning, they turn into a witch! They throw potions to attack you and drink potions to heal themselves, so are hard to fight.

BLAZE: Friendly? Not at all

Blazes live in Nether fortresses. Their attacks set you on fire, but you'll have to kill them to complete the game, as you need the blaze rods they carry to find strongholds.

GUARDIAN: Friendly? You wish

Guardians are powerful enemies that spawn in ocean monuments. They make it hard to retrieve the treasure inside because the lasers they shoot are strong and hard to dodge.

Feed an ocelot fish to turn it into a tame cat

OCELOT: Friendly? Potentially

Ocelots spawn in jungles and will mostly just run away from you, but convince them to eat fish and they'll turn into a tame cat, which can scare creepers away!

SHULKER: Friendly? Nah

Shulkers live in the End and disguise themselves as purpur blocks. If you get too close, they'll shoot you with their levitation projectile, which makes you float upwards.

GET STARTED IN MINECRAFT!

Just got your hands on Minecraft for the very first time? Then these tips are perfect for you, to help you on your adventuring way!

How Much Wood?

Wherever you start in Minecraft, you should be able to find wood close by. If you can't see any, just head for anything that looks green (except a cactus). The first thing you should try to do in any game is stock up on logs. These can be collected quite easily without tools. You can then convert them into planks and sticks. Planks and sticks will allow you to create wooden tools and a crafting table, giving you the basic tools you need to survive in the game.

Those trees will be a good source of wood

Wood becomes planks...

...planks become sticks...

The spawn point for this world. Roomy!

First thing to do in any game is stock up on logs

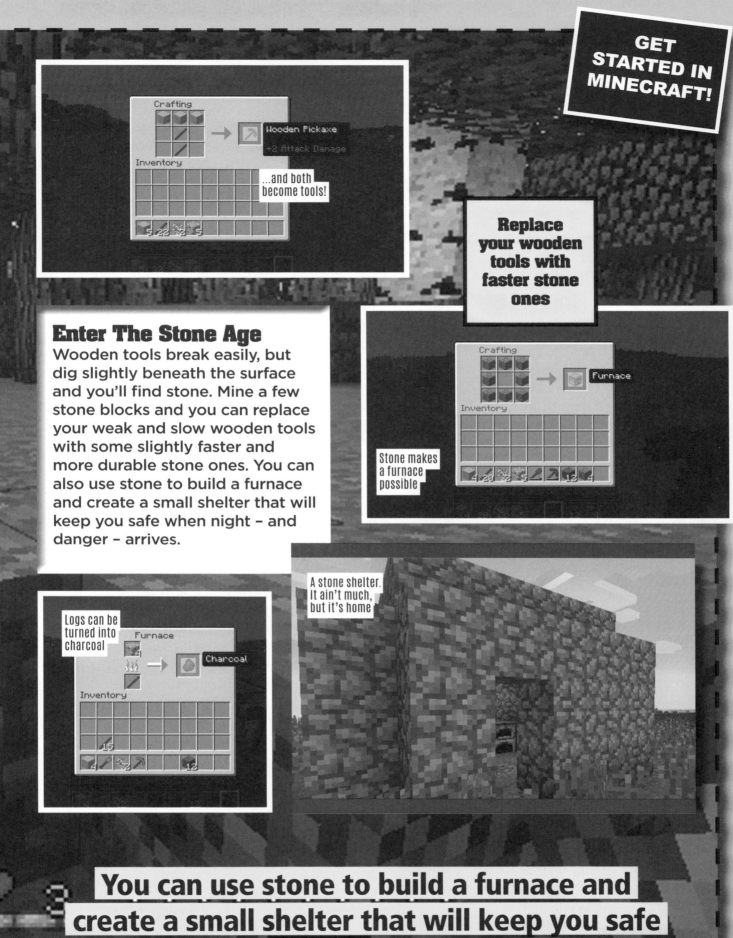

Crafting

Wooden Pickaxe
+2 Attack Damage

Inventory

...and both become tools!

Replace your wooden tools with faster stone ones

Crafting

Furnace

Inventory

Stone makes a furnace possible

Enter The Stone Age

Wooden tools break easily, but dig slightly beneath the surface and you'll find stone. Mine a few stone blocks and you can replace your weak and slow wooden tools with some slightly faster and more durable stone ones. You can also use stone to build a furnace and create a small shelter that will keep you safe when night – and danger – arrives.

Logs can be turned into charcoal

Furnace

Charcoal

Inventory

A stone shelter. It ain't much, but it's home

You can use stone to build a furnace and create a small shelter that will keep you safe when night – and danger – arrives

Coal Powered

A fully lit shelter is safe, because enemies can only spawn in the dark. This early in the game, the only way to keep your shelter lit is to use torches. If you can see some coal in a cliff, mine it as soon as possible. If you can't, you can smelt some wooden logs in your furnace to create charcoal. Remember that you can use almost anything that burns as a fuel source in a furnace. Planks and sticks are fine.

When the log is fully smelted, you'll get a piece of charcoal. Coal and charcoal can be combined with sticks to make torches, which will stop enemies from spawning in a closed-off shelter.

You can use almost anything that burns as fuel

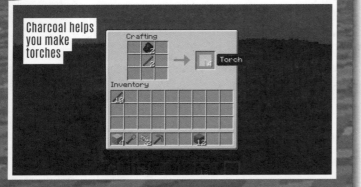

Charcoal helps you make torches

Peace In Our Time

If you're struggling to get started because of the attacking zombie hordes, you may want to change the difficulty level to Peaceful until things calm down. There are no enemies in Peaceful and you won't have to find food, so you can figure things out at your own pace. Remember there are some items you can only get by killing monsters, so don't stay in Peaceful forever!

Lunch Time

At the start of the game, you won't have time to grow crops, so the quickest way to get food is to find and kill an animal. Pigs, cows and chickens all drop food when killed. Cook it in a furnace and you'll get even more health when you eat it!

Although you may find some other edible items, don't rely on them to feed you. Most can't be eaten without being crafted into something else. Mushrooms, wheat, cocoa beans, eggs, sugar and pumpkins can only be eaten if combined with other ingredients in a recipe. Apples can be eaten raw, but you have to destroy up to 200 oak leaves to find one. Melons can be crafted into melon slices then eaten, but only spawn in jungle biomes. Potatoes and carrots can be eaten, but they are only found in village farms.

Don't Wander Off

Compasses always point to the place you first appeared in the world. It's a good idea to build your base close to the place you start so that if you ever get lost or die, you know where to return to.

Build your base close to the place you start

Cows are sources of food and leather

Bed Time

If you make it through the first night, make sure you don't have to stay awake all night again. Explore grassland and hills to find some sheep. Kill them and take their wool. When you have three wool blocks, return to your base and craft the wool blocks with three wood planks to make a bed. Beds let you skip the nights and set a respawn point. If you die, you reappear next to the last bed you slept in.

A bed helps you skip dangerous nights

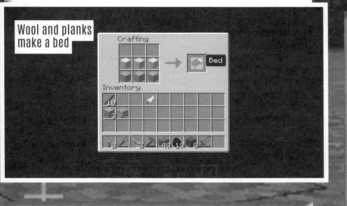

Wool and planks make a bed

Go Adventuring

Once you've got weapons and armour, you can explore properly. It's too early to make a compass, so leave yourself pointers so you can find your way back home. Torches are a good choice because you can easily see them at night and from a distance. Your next plan should be to head underground. Look for openings and caves that lead you beneath the surface.

Protect Yourself

You've already got everything you need to make a stone sword – sticks and stone – so you're halfway to protecting yourself. Next, you need to make armour. You can't make armour out of wood or stone, but you can make it out of leather. Kill some cows and create as much armour as possible (you need 24 pieces for a full suit, but just four will make some leather boots).

Collect a little at a time, and return home often

Iron Man

When you go underground, stock up on coal, but also iron ore. Once you have five or six pieces, head back to base and smelt it into iron ingots. You can craft these into iron tools, which are strong enough to let you do some real exploring! Don't get greedy. Low health, weak weapons and poor armour make fighting difficult, so don't lose all of your hard work by trying to collect a lot of resources in one go.

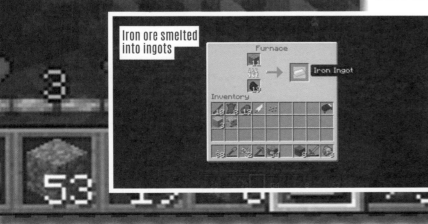

Iron ore smelted into ingots

AMAZING MINECRAFT BUILDS

It's possible to make just about anything in Minecraft if you have the imagination, but every so often we stumble on creations that really blow our minds. Here is our top 12 countdown of amazing Minecraft builds, from sprawling cities to entire puzzle games created inside our favourite pastime.

All feathers lie at or near a point of intersection
Conclusive proof of dual wave/particle nature of the chicken

All in the name of science, of course!

11 Underground 2 survival map

The scenario behind this huge survival map is that the world's temperature has dropped so low you've had to make your way underground to scratch out a living. But surviving here is just as tough, and this 2,000 x 2,000 block map contains all kinds of trials to overcome, plus a lost city to uncover.
tinyurl.com/MCW2017Build11

12 Large Hadron Collider - with chickens

You may have heard of the Large Hadron Collider, a huge machine dedicated to smashing together particles and examining the results. The real thing is the largest machine in the world, but spoonmonkeyuk has managed to build a scale replica. And because this is Minecraft, it smashes together chickens not particles!
tinyurl.com/MCW2017Build12

One of the best survival maps ever made

will be in the . . .

Asgard in the making

10 Asgard

Here's a massive project to recreate the realm of Asgard, as seen in Marvel's *Thor* films. While it's still a work in progress, creator Jake_Scanlan has already made about a dozen buildings, including the familiar Asgard Temple with its jutting gold spires. Best of all, he's already built the Bifrost, the rainbow-coloured bridge that stretches between Asgard and Midgard.

tinyurl.com/MCW2017Build10

9 House In The Water

Now here's a construction that really caught our eye. It's one thing cutting a sprawling lair into the ground or putting together a dwelling in a tree, but building something as complex as this under the water without it getting flooded! That's something else entirely. Darkscour's house in the water is a huge web of rooms made from stone and wood. Best of all, there's a glass ceiling so you can see all the water from the ocean floor. Brilliant!

tinyurl.com/MCW2017Build9

How does the whole place not flood? Amazing!

How cool is that glass ceiling?!

Constructed from 4.5 million blocks!

7 Tower Of Babel

If this colossal skyscraper were real, it would be the tallest building in the world. Where the Burj Khalifa (scaled by Tom Cruise in the film *Mission: Impossible - Ghost Protocol!*) stands 828 metres tall, this Tower Of Babel tops out at a dizzying 1036 metres. Okay, so the Minecraft building has fewer floors – 100 to the Burj Khalifa's 154 – but it's nevertheless built from approximately seven million blocks and lit up by 90,000 lights. We're just glad we don't have to pay the electricity bill.
tinyurl.com/MCW2017Build7

8 Titan City

This is one of the most incredible bits of building we've seen in Minecraft. Made by art student Duncan Parcells, Titan City is constructed from 4.5 million blocks, and took him an astonishing two years to build. What's even more amazing is that Duncan actually put each block in place by hand. The city has roads, pavements, street lights and bridges, and some of its skyscrapers even have stairs, lifts and furnishings. To be honest, we're not sure how he managed to build it all without getting completely lost.
tinyurl.com/MCW2017Build8

Now that's what you call a tower, ready to be smited

The tower is 100 floors high, consists of over seven million blocks and has around 90,000 lights

Neat way of keeping out mobs

5 Redstone Computer

A few decades ago, the tech behind this computer would have been cutting edge. But user LPG has spent the last couple of years building a computer inside Minecraft. It's one of the most sophisticated computers we've seen in the game: you can play Noughts and Crosses and a trivia game on it, and it even comes with its own wireless keyboard and mouse. LPG's adding to it all the time, too. A recent update on YouTube shows the machine browsing the web.

tinyurl.com/MCW2017Build5

6 Lava Castle

Moats are a great means of protecting your property, but how about surrounding your dwelling with a circle of scalding hot lava? That's exactly what you'll find around this great-looking castle, which even has lava cascading down its medieval-style towers.

tinyurl.com/MCWBuild6

A working computer within Minecraft?!

HELLO, M_

You can play Noughts and Crosses and a trivia game on it, and it even comes with its own wireless keyboard and mouse

The original Star Wars - in Minecraft form!

3 Prismatic puzzle game

Here's an ingenious build that turns Minecraft into a single-player puzzle game. Prismatic presents the player with a series of intricately designed rooms, which have to be navigated through by manipulating coloured beams of light with glass cubes. It all looks simple enough to begin with, but Prismatic soon becomes a brain-meltingly challenging network of interlocking puzzles. One of the best single-player games we've seen so far in Minecraft? Most definitely!

tinyurl.com/MCW2017Build3

4 The entirety of Star Wars: A New Hope

We've seen some complex buildings and even cities constructed in Minecraft, but what about a shot-for-shot remake of *Star Wars* made entirely from blocks? According to its creator, the fan-film has been four years in the making. You'll need the original DVD or Blu-ray in your disc drive to provide the sound, which should sync perfectly with this lovingly recreated space fantasy.

tinyurl.com/MCW2017Build4

One of the best single-player games in Minecraft

It all looks simple enough to begin with, but Prismatic soon becomes a brain-meltingly challenging network of interlocking puzzles

This Mega Gargantua robot is controllable

2 Giant battle robot

There's something vaguely scary about this giant robot, which looms up over the player like a hulking skyscraper. The most impressive thing about this four-legged monster? You can actually control it. According to its creator Cubehamster, the project took around 60 hours to build, and just looking at the number of intricate moving parts it uses to move around, we can see why. The robot isn't just mobile, either – it's also armed with a variety of weapons, including TNT cannons and bomb launchers.

tinyurl.com/MCW2017Build2

1 A working printer

Now this one really is clever. You start by placing coloured blocks in a large chest to create a picture, and then YouTube user ACtennis AC's printer creates a full-scale version of that image. To demonstrate, he draws a creeper face with lime and black wool. When he's finished, he closes the chest, and the printer gradually recreates the image out of large woollen blocks. This is one build we could play around with for ages.

tinyurl.com/MCW2017Build1

A very clever build!

The most impressive thing about this four-legged monster? You can actually control it

LAVA RUSH

Using the grass blocks, try to find the way from the start to the dimond Ore. Do not fall into the lava!

START

FINISH

WORDSEARCH

W	X	L	D	A	V	C	W	V	L	M	L	C	Z	J	S	X	O	V	S	S	M	J	B	H
C	U	F	R	N	S	H	E	E	P	R	I	F	R	D	A	Z	B	G	P	T	E	T	R	Z
M	U	S	H	R	O	O	M	S	V	L	I	I	X	A	S	T	S	X	O	J	E	A	A	R
M	P	T	G	M	M	M	N	U	A	P	L	F	K	U	F	R	I	C	R	E	R	V	Y	D
X	E	L	P	O	B	L	A	V	Z	T	D	T	U	A	J	T	D	B	T	Q	G	W	E	I
B	P	F	J	Z	B	Q	A	I	C	Z	U	I	R	N	H	J	I	L	A	V	S	H	I	M
F	U	C	Q	L	X	J	K	B	D	S	X	C	I	U	B	R	A	N	L	X	N	Q	U	J
T	N	E	M	T	N	A	H	C	N	E	E	B	K	J	B	Z	N	B	G	O	K	N	A	A
D	Y	Y	Y	S	Z	V	K	M	A	N	F	W	Q	H	S	T	T	W	L	L	E	B	R	R
F	Z	W	L	A	A	I	T	F	I	R	R	Z	O	Y	M	U	K	P	G	X	S	J	W	D
D	B	C	K	H	J	I	P	M	K	P	R	N	U	S	V	G	J	N	A	S	B	O	M	K
O	U	Y	I	G	B	V	P	H	L	V	F	E	T	K	M	A	A	B	J	V	J	I	D	H
B	Z	Z	J	E	B	U	B	U	J	W	D	C	H	E	F	J	Z	A	A	C	L	Q	S	V
D	C	T	S	T	V	X	H	A	Z	Y	C	G	W	T	O	V	A	A	C	E	Y	S	D	A
M	T	O	W	Q	R	P	K	I	L	U	F	R	G	M	E	C	W	B	W	N	E	G	L	L
E	X	C	W	K	C	E	G	L	R	P	E	T	S	C	T	N	I	D	Q	O	W	C	S	E
R	E	P	E	E	R	C	D	E	K	A	L	X	C	B	E	W	Z	M	Z	T	P	N	B	X
E	M	O	I	B	D	O	D	N	L	Q	B	I	R	D	H	P	G	N	K	S	B	X	X	O
Y	K	H	Z	D	Q	S	C	M	E	I	W	M	X	J	C	W	Z	B	K	W	V	R	N	I
Z	O	N	A	G	T	U	S	E	B	I	E	F	P	Q	K	N	D	A	V	O	Y	C	I	P
V	Y	E	H	O	E	Q	C	Q	L	L	A	W	L	V	D	Q	F	N	I	L	S	E	K	G
G	O	A	N	E	T	H	E	R	O	O	W	G	L	A	K	P	V	S	V	G	Y	C	P	F
T	B	E	G	J	L	T	I	G	K	C	T	Y	M	R	G	M	V	X	V	L	J	I	M	T
I	Y	J	P	D	T	M	W	X	A	D	U	L	T	I	L	C	Z	X	X	G	F	Q	U	W
L	X	C	G	I	L	C	J	M	I	I	F	U	N	A	T	O	A	D	Y	R	W	Q	P	R

ALEX	ENCHANTMENT	LAVA	NETHER	PUMPKIN
BIOME	ENDER	MINECRAFT	NETHERRACK	REALMS
CRAFTING	GHAST	MOBS	OBSIDIAN	REDSTONE
CREEPER	GLOWSTONE	MOJANG	OCELOT	SHEEP
DIAMOND	GOLEM	MUSHROOMS	PORTAL	STEVE

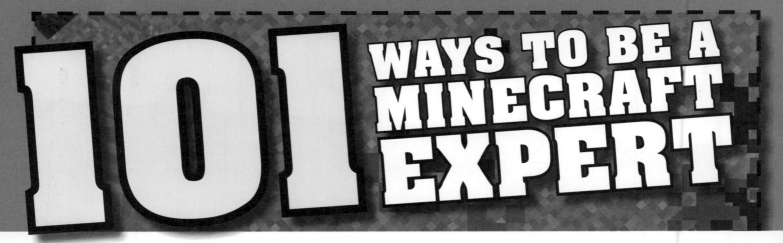

101 WAYS TO BE A MINECRAFT EXPERT

You can learn how to play Minecraft in hours, but becoming an expert can take months, if not years! Even people who play every day might not know the tricks and shortcuts you need to play like a pro, which is why we've put together a selection of tips, advice and facts that can help you take your Minecraft skills to the next level!

BUILDING & DECORATION

1 When you're decorating your base, remember that you can put more than just flowers in flower pots. They can also hold mushrooms, grass and ferns, saplings (which never grow) and even cacti!

Build in the side of a cliff for maximum security

2 Consider building your base in the side of a mountain. There'll be fewer ways for mobs to sneak up on you, and you'll get easy access to minerals like coal and iron ore without having to travel deep underground.

3 If you want a fire that never goes out, set Netherrack on fire. You can use this technique to create an incinerator, build a working fireplace or just use it as some dramatic decoration.

Set Netherrack alight and it burns forever

4 If you want to light underwater, use glowstone blocks or (if you haven't reached the Nether yet) Jack 'O' Lanterns. Both of

Glowstone works underwater

these blocks emit light even stronger than a torch, and can't be extinguished underwater.

5 You can build a base in the Nether, but don't ever place a bed there. It will explode like TNT if you try to sleep in it and do a LOT of damage!

A recipe for disaster

6 You can easily create an infinite water pool by putting four water source blocks in a 2x2 square. If you collect any water using a bucket, it will instantly regenerate.

7 You can use half-size blocks like stone slabs to create staircases with a more gentle incline than actual staircase blocks provide.

8 Carpet tiles don't block light, so if you want to make a room look bright without having lights in the way, just lay carpet on top of glowstone, redstone lanterns or sea lanterns. It looks a little odd at first!

CRAFTING

9 You can make copies of books and maps (either for backups or sharing with other players) by crafting them with a blank version of what they are.

10 You can place a clock inside an item frame to create a wall clock, which lets you see how long you've got until it gets dark (or light!) without taking up valuable space in your inventory.

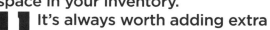
Put a clock in a frame and it can hang on the wall

11 It's always worth adding extra lighting to a village to keep mobs away. You could even build a defensive wall around it if you want to keep the villagers safe!

12 Don't waste glass blocks by using them as windows. Six glass blocks make 16 glass panes, so it's more efficient to craft them than place them.

13 You can till coarse dirt into regular dirt using a hoe, and you can create four blocks of coarse dirt by mixing two gravel blocks and two regular dirt blocks.

14 Brew gunpowder into a water bottle and you can use the resulting splash water bottle/potion to put out fires by throwing it at the flames – even in the Nether.

A splash water bottle puts out fire on up to five blocks

15 Elytra can't be crafted, but you can repair them by using leather on an anvil. Four leather will completely repair one set of elytra.

Elytra can be repaired easily with leather

16 Don't repair enchanted items on a crafting grid, as you'll lose the enchantments. Use an anvil and raw materials instead.

17 Craft resources like coal, redstone dust, clay and snow into blocks for easy storage. You can carry up to nine times as much in a single inventory slot this way.

18 Crafting minecart rails takes up a lot of resources and time, so when you stumble across an abandoned mine be sure to take as many of the unused rails as you can carry back to the surface with you.

Get rails from abandoned mines

ANIMALS

19 Don't bother killing baby animals when you come across them. They don't drop anything – not even experience – when they die, so there's no reason to waste your weapons on them. Wait until they're fully grown.

20 Wolf packs will actively hunt other animals, but they'll leave you alone unless you injure them. Hurt one, though, and the whole pack will come for you, so take care!

21 Rather than dyeing wool, find a sheep and dye it. This permanently changes the wool colour even after the wool regrows, so you can keep shearing your sheep for an unending supply of coloured wool.

Dye sheep, not wool blocks

22 Most animals will follow you if you hold a certain type of food. For chickens it's grain, for rabbits and pigs it's carrots, and so on. Use this behaviour to lead lots of animals at once so you can pen them in.

23 Always leave at least two animals in a herd alive so that you can breed more if you need to. Killing the whole herd is fine in the short

One animal can't replenish a herd alone

term, but you'll regret it when you need the resources!

24 If you walk too far from a tamed wolf it teleports next to you, so don't worry about losing it during a fight!

A tame wolf will always teleport near you

25 Horses, donkeys and mules can eat hay bales, healing up to 10 hearts. They're by far the most efficient way to restore your ride's health, so make sure you keep a few near your base and feed one to your horse when you return.

Horses can heal by eating hay

26 Feeding sugar to a horse has a variety of different effects. It heals adult horses, makes smaller ones grow faster and also helps wild ones tame a bit more easily.

MOBS

27 The moon's phases affect how mobs spawn, so pay attention. Full moons are the most dangerous. You'll see more slimes and stronger mobs, possibly with enchanted weapons, so prepare for a big fight!

Full moons raise the chance of mobs spawning with equipment

28 On harder modes, zombies will look for and try to break down wooden doors. Use steel doors activated by a button to keep them out – they can't ever break through metal.

Zombies attacking a door

29 You can tell what profession a zombie villager had when it was alive, and you can use that to help you decide whether to kill it or try curing it. They might make a useful trading partner!

30 If you want to fight the ender dragon again, craft an End crystal using an eye of ender, a ghast tear and seven glass blocks, then place it on the exit portal in the End. This will summon a new dragon.

31 Once you've built a portal, there's a small chance of zombie pigmen spawning near it, so make sure it's built somewhere out of the way, if not fenced in completely. You don't want any nasty surprises!

32 Despite their short appearance, baby zombies are faster and more powerful than regular zombies, and can fit through smaller gaps, so take them out first! Otherwise, you might miss them while you're trying to fend off the larger ones!

Baby zombies can also ride chickens

33 The first time you get into a fight with a blaze, use a golden or enchanted apple to temporarily raise your stats so that you're less likely to die. After that point, you can use blaze powder to craft fire resistance potions, which will keep you safe.

When you fight a blaze, bring a golden apple

CONTINUED ON PAGE 38!

25

THE BEST MINECRAFT YOUTUBERS!

If you're looking for brilliant tips, amazing maps and epic Let's Play videos, there are loads of great videos on YouTube that are worth checking out! Here are some of our favourite channels, but make sure you check with an adult before trying them out!

One of the most popular Minecraft YouTubers

SETHBLING
www.youtube.com/user/sethbling

The best thing about SethBling's YouTube channel is the amazing inventions he puts together, plus he shows you how he makes them! There's more than just Minecraft to be found, but you can probably guess where we spend most of our time! His Space Invaders Minecraft game in particular is brilliant!

MR STAMPY CAT
www.youtube.com/user/stampylonghead

The brilliant StampyLongHead is one of the most popular Minecraft YouTubers, and rightly so! Stampy uploads at least one new Minecraft video to his channel every day, and he also covers other games. But it's his Let's Play videos that we love the most. It always makes us smile when he announces, "Hellloooooooo! This is Stampy!"

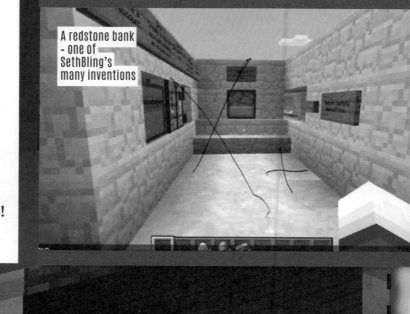

A redstone bank - one of SethBling's many inventions

Become a Noodler today!

THINKNOODLES
www.youtube.com/user/
InsidersNetwork

You get lots of exploring with ThinkNoodles, a channel that's mostly dedicated to Minecraft videos! In particular, there are tonnes of Minecraft role play adventures, which are loads of fun. Plus, it's very rare you get to the end of a ThinkNoodles video without having laughed yourself silly!

THE DIAMOND MINECART
www.youtube.com/user/
TheDiamondMinecart

You'll find a new Minecraft upload every day at The Diamond Minecart, a YouTube channel that explores every corner of the game! Dan is a brilliant host, and you can see his face in the corner as he talks over what's on screen. You may know him better as DanTDM!

The epic DanTDM!

SKY
www.youtube.com/user/
SkyDoesMinecraft

You'll find Minecraft role play, lots of custom minigames, server games and hundreds of videos at Sky's Minecraft channel, which already has millions of subscribers! We think Sky's really funny, and we think you will, too!

Loads of laughs with Sky!

iBallisticSquid in action!

SIMPLEBLAZE
www.youtube.com/user/
xSimpleBlaze

A channel themed around medieval builds, so if you like castles and villages from the olden days you'll love it. Tutorials include houses, towers, churches, blacksmiths, stables, barns and more. If you like ambitious building projects, there's plenty to keep you busy!

IBALLISTICSQUID
www.youtube.com/user/
iBallisticSquid

One of Stampy's friends, iBallisticSquid (love the name) has a packed YouTube channel, where he plays Minecraft on his Xbox and gleefully chats over the games! There are lots of brilliant challenges in his videos, too, and sometimes he even does videos with Stampy!

For all your medieval build needs

THEBAJANCANADIAN
youtube.com/user/
TheBajanCanadian

One of the funniest Minecraft YouTube channels we've seen. Canadian Mitch's videos include minigames, challenges and songs, and the whole thing might make you invest in a black and red checked hoodie!

Loads of tutorials and tips

MINECRAFT UNIVERSE
www.youtube.com/user/
MinecraftUniverse

If you're anything like us, you'll learn lots from the tutorials at Minecraft Universe. Hosted by TrueMU, we recommend you check out his brilliant parkour videos. It's also worth going through his collection of tips.

Check out that hoodie!

Become a cute recruit today!

stacysays

MARICRAFT
tinyurl.com/mw-maricraft

Every Monday, Mari posts a new Minecraft video, and her Let's Play uploads are brilliant. She plays across all sorts of maps, and has some amazing battles in them! Her videos tend to be quite short, too, so MariCraft is perfect when you want to sneak one episode in before bedtime!

AMY LEE
www.youtube.com/user/amyleethirty3

A channel run by AmyLee33, who posts a new video every day! There are lots of series running, which go up every week, including a Crazy Craft series that goes up at weekends, Mermaid Mondays (every Monday, obviously!) and her own special series, Amy's Land of Love, which is focused around Amy Lee's original character, Princess Amy.

WHEN ANIMALS ATTACK! (Maricraft)

Home of brilliant Let's Play videos

enshire left the game

A little yellow duck who loves playing games

Quack - Channel Trailer

SQAISHEY QUACK
www.youtube.com/user/sqaishey

Sqaishey Quack follows the adventures of a yellow duck. A new video goes up most days, and you can watch videos of the Cloud Nest Sqaishey has built, Treasure Tracker mode, stranded modes, and an attempt to play in Hardcore mode!

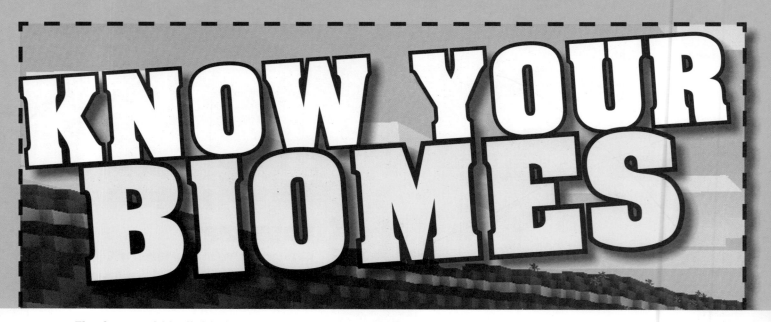

KNOW YOUR BIOMES

The Overworld is divided into different types of landscape, which are known as "biomes". Each one has its own special features, from plants to animals to structures. And with this handy guide, you can find out exactly what they are!

A roofed forest with a huge mushroom

Plains

Plains are flat and thick with tall grass. They spawn large numbers of peaceful mobs and are a common place to find villages. Sunflower plains, as the name suggests, are full of sunflowers.

Forest

Forest biomes are dense with trees, usually oak, dark oak or birch. Mushrooms are also quite common due to the shade provided by the leaves. Roofed forests are very dense and contain huge mushrooms mixed in with the trees, and they're often dark enough for mobs to spawn even during the day!

Flower Forest

Flower forests contain a lot of different flower types, most of which you can only find there. Lilac, rose bush and peony only appear in flower forests.

Swampland

Swampland is a mixture of dark green islands and shallow, greenish water filled with lily pads. Vines hang off the trees here, and you can find lots of red and brown mushrooms. Witch huts and blue orchid flowers can only be found here, and at night slimes spawn above ground.

Beach

Beaches form at the edge of oceans and replace the biome with sand (or gravel). They're a good place to find sand and sandstone.

Flower forests grow lots of rare blooms

Beaches form at the edge of oceans

Stone beaches are dangerous due to their long drops

Extreme Hills

This biome contains huge, steep mountains wit[h] few trees, but lots of caves. [You] only find emerald ore here, [be] careful when mining as it's a[lso the] only place where silverfish can be encountered outside of strongholds. Extreme hills+ has more trees.

Mushroom islands are hard to find, but very

Extreme hills are steep and dangerous

Stone Beach

You can only find stone beaches where mountain biomes meet ocean biomes. They're good places to build lookout points, but difficult to farm due to the lack of greenery.

Taiga

A warm forest of birch trees and small ferns. Taiga biomes are the best place to find wolves. The mega taiga spawns very tall, thick trees, mossy boulders and podzol, a rare dirt type that doesn't grow grass. You might also find the cold taiga biome, which is the same as the normal one except snowy, and the mega spruce taiga, which has leafier trees.

The rarer mega taiga biome

Ice Plains

Large, empty and icy, ice plains are difficult places to survive because they have few trees. It snows instead of rains, and you will find frozen rivers and snowy beaches here and nowhere else. Ice plains contain igloos and very rarely contain ice spikes.

Ice plains have lots of snow, but not much else!

Jungle biomes are incredibly dense

Jungle

This biome consists of tall, thick trees with dense leaf cover. Melons and cocoa pods can be found exclusively here, and it's the only place ocelots spawn. The trees are normally covered in vines, and you can only find jungle temples here.

...y Safe!

Savanna

The warm grasslands of the savanna are the only place where you can find acacia trees, and the second of two biomes in which horses spawn naturally, and the third where villages spawn. Savanna plateau forms tall hills with flat tops.

Mesa

One of the rarest biomes, mesas are desert variants composed of red sand, hardened clay and stained clay. They're for mining clay and the only place you

You can find wells, cacti and dead bushes in deserts

Deep oceans are the only place you can find monuments

Mushroom Island

Mushroom islands are only found in the ocean and are topped with mycelium, not dirt. They're covered in mushrooms and huge mushrooms, and are the only place to find mooshrooms. No other mobs will spawn here.

Desert

Deserts are carpeted in sand above a base of sandstone. They're free from almost all animal and plant life, though rabbits do spawn, and cacti and dead bushes are only found here. You can also find sugar cane, desert temples and wells.

Villages appear in savanna biomes

can find red sand, but their rarity means it's hard to rely on them. Mesas also have a plateau variant, and in Pocket Edition it's possible to find gold and mines at ground level.

Ocean/Deep Ocean

Ocean biomes largely consist of water around 15 blocks above the ocean floor, which is usually made of sand. Deep ocean is twice as deep and the ocean floor is usually gravel. This is the only place you can find monuments.

Mesas are full of clay

Snow falls in cold biomes, carpeting exposed blocks with snow

Hills Variants

Hills can be generated in deserts, forests, taiga, jungle and ice plains biomes, and aren't as steep as the mountains generated by M variant biomes.

Biome Achievements

There are 61 biomes in total, although many are just temperature or relief variants of existing ones. If you've completed the achievement "The End?", you can get the "Adventuring Time" achievement by visiting 36 biomes on the PC or 17 biomes on the Xbox or Pocket Edition.

Temperature

All biomes have a hidden temperature value that determines whether it rains, snows or stays dry. Biomes with similar temperatures are more likely to appear near one another. The temperature inside a biome also drops as you get higher above sea level.

Savanna M biomes reach extreme heights

M Variants

Some biomes have an "M" variant. They're identical to the normal version, but they also have steep hills. You can find M variants of taiga, cold taiga, extreme hills, extreme hills+, plains, swampland, jungle, jungle edge M, forest, forest hills, roofed forest, desert, savanna and plateau biomes.

The Nether is technically a biome...

...and so is the End!

Forest hills biomes are easy to get lost in!

Other Dimensions

Technically, the Nether and the End are separate biomes. Despite this, neither will appear in the Overworld and they can only be accessed by portals, although they do count towards the biome achievements!

SHOWING OFF YOUR EPIC LOOT

So you've crafted yourself loads of epic loot, but what's the best way to show off your sweet gear? Join us as we present the coolest-looking loot on display – in item frames!

After several nights spent deep underground, battling slimes and hunting for emeralds, it's nice to have something attractive to come home to. And if your efforts are largely devoted to crafting the most epic loot, and you're not that fussed about interior design, item frames are the perfect way to display your gear.

Armour

If you've crafted diamond armour it's clear you're a powerful warrior, and if you've crafted gold armour it's obvious you've got resources to burn, so why not show off a bit?

What to wear?

Although you can also exhibit your spare armour on armour stancs, we think it looks better in an item frame. If you disagree, you can still use item frames to enhance your armour display!

Horse armour also looks great in an item frame

Item frames are the perfect way to display your gear

Enchanted items

Any item that has an enchantment applied to it has a glowing effect, and these effects still appear when the item is then placed into an item frame!

Potions, enchantment books, even the super-rare Nether star – which is obtained when killing a wither – are all excellent items to show off on your wall.

A Nether star, splash potion, and enchanted golden apple

Glowing effects still show when item placed in a frame

Rare blocks

If you've spent enough time enchanting items, you may have in your possession a pickaxe (diamond, of course) with the Silk Touch enchantment. This allows you to mine blocks that otherwise aren't available outside of Creative mode.

What better way to spice up your loot displays than with some of these mega-rare blocks?

Emerald and diamond blocks look particularly spectacular!

Heads

Here's a grisly option: the severed heads of your enemies!

It's possible to obtain the heads of zombies, skeletons and creepers in Survival mode. To do so, you need to engineer a situation where these enemies are killed by the explosion of a charged creeper.

What's a charged creeper? Er, it's a creeper that's been struck by lightning! Lightning strikes only occur during thunderstorms, and where those strikes happen is entirely random.

Still, if you're able to obtain these heads, they look great on your wall!

Clocks

Clocks are awesome items to put in an item frame because they show the day/night cycle, just as they do in an inventory slot.

Place these anywhere underground where you can't easily see the sky!

Getting a-head in life, eh?

A charged creeper

Place clocks anywhere where you can't easily see the sky

Crafting

How to craft a clock

Other items

Few people realise it, but sponges are actually one of the rarest items in Minecraft. They can only be found in ocean monuments or as elder guardian drops. Sadly, they don't look very exciting in a frame.

All sorts of other items do look cool in an item frame, however, including TNT, ender chests (mined with Silk Touch), cake and even pufferfish!

Arranging your item frames

How cool something looks on its own is one thing, but what about creating a whole wall of item frames? But where do you start?

The best way to approach this is to experiment. Try different materials for your walls, including different woods, types of stone, fences or something more unusual.

You can place and remove item frames freely, so experiment with different patterns until you find a layout that you like. Go nuts!

Sponges may not look much, but they're very rare

How cool does that pufferfish look?!

Use windows to allow natural light onto your display

Try putting an item frame over a torch, then adding an anvil to the frame to make this cool torch-holder!

A simple criss-cross pattern looks great. Also, do you like our fancy redstone lamp?

Feel free to experiment with different patterns

This entire building is a gallery full of item frame displays

37

101 WAYS TO BE A MINECRAFT EXPERT PART 2

FOOD & PLANTS

Large mushrooms break into smaller ones

34 It's hard to grow mushrooms, but if you use bone meal to turn them into large mushrooms you can harvest up to two mushrooms per block, and an average large mushroom will yield around 14 small ones. You'll never go hungry again!

35 Cocoa pods only grow naturally on jungle trees, but as soon as you find one you can farm pods on any tree trunk. It doesn't have to be part of a tree!

36 When you find a flower forest, stock up on rare plants you can't get anywhere else. Then, you'll always have them to hand if you need a unique decoration or source of dye.

Flower forests contain rare coloured plants

37 Large trees, like dark oak and jungle trees, can be grown by planting four saplings together then fertilising one with bone meal.

38 Cake blocks are the only block type you can eat directly. It makes them good for storing food nearby.

39 Cooked steak and pork chops are common food items that restore a lot of hunger points, so stock up on them, especially early in the game when you'll lose health quickly.

40 Save clownfish for taming ocelots. They have almost no other use and restore only a tiny amount of health if eaten, but will please ocelots as much as any other fish.

Tame ocelots

41 Jungle saplings drop half as often as other saplings, and one jungle tree may not drop any saplings. You'll have to collect four saplings and grow a giant tree if you want to farm them!

42 Drinking milk buckets cures potion effects, so try and make sure you keep one with you in case you encounter a witch. Remember to fill it back up once you've used it, though!

43 If you want to clear things like grass, flowers and ferns, drop a water source block so that it spreads in all directions, then pick it back up. The ground will then be washed clean.

TOOLS & WEAPONS

44 Remember that armour only protects you from physical attacks. Fire, fall damage and drowning aren't any less dangerous, although you can apply enchantments to armour pieces to make them that way.

45 Wear a pumpkin as a helmet to stop endermen noticing and attacking you at night, although it's hard to see out of!

Wear a pumpkin

46 You can repair rare chainmail armour by using iron ingots on an anvil. Chainmail armour is slightly weaker than iron armour, but holds better enchantments.

47 Enchant books rather than items, then combine the book with the target tool/armour on an anvil. It costs more, but you won't end up with enchantments you don't like on your valuable equipment.

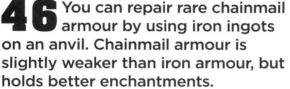
Enchant books rather than items

48 Use shears on cobwebs to cut them down quickly and collect string. You can also use a sword, but this takes longer and is a waste of its durability!

Use shears on cobwebs to get string

49 Learn to use the most appropriate tool to break blocks. Wooden blocks usually break fastest with an axe, stone with a pickaxe, and dirt with a spade.

50 Place your favourite type of arrow in your offhand inventory slot and your bow will prioritise those arrows; otherwise, it takes them from the lowest numbered inventory slot.

51 You can combine a banner with a shield to transfer the pattern onto it. You can't remove the pattern or apply a new one, though, so make sure you do it right!

52 Shields can't be enchanted directly, but you can apply Unbreaking to them using an anvil and enchanted book.

You can't enchant shields directly

53 Fishing during a rainstorm decreases the time you wait to get a bite. Fishing in water that isn't exposed to open sky increases the time it takes to get a bite.

FIGHTING

54 When fighting the wither, create a distraction by building lots of golems. They can't do much damage, but the wither will attack anything it sees, which will give you more time to attack it.

The wither can be distracted

55 Destroy ender crystals with a bow and arrow while the ender dragon is healing itself with them and you'll deal a lot of damage to the dragon.

Destroy ender crystals as the dragon heals to hurt it

56 If you sprint and attack a creeper, you should cause enough knockback to get out of the way so it doesn't explode!

57 Shulkers have very high armour when inside their shells. Wait until they peep out before attacking, because you provoke the other shulkers into attacking you when you hit one of them.

Shulkers have lots of armour

58 Don't waste arrows trying to hit endermen. They'll teleport away long before the arrow gets anywhere near them! You have to wait until they teleport near you, then hit them with a melee attack if you want to do damage. Or you can always sneak up on them while wearing a pumpkin!

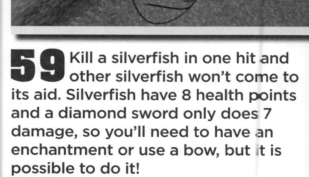

Don't waste arrows trying to hit endermen

59 Kill a silverfish in one hit and other silverfish won't come to its aid. Silverfish have 8 health points and a diamond sword only does 7 damage, so you'll need to have an enchantment or use a bow, but it is possible to do it!

60 If villagers get injured by mobs, you can heal them by using a splash/lingering potion of healing or by trading an item with them. It's faster than waiting for a new villager to spawn and/or grow to adulthood!

61 Monster spawners are rare and can be hard to find, but destroying one gets you more immediate experience than anything else in the game other than killing a boss creature.

EXPLORING

62 It can be useful to carry a bed with you when exploring the Overworld so that you can wall yourself up and skip nights. Just be careful to stay alive. If the last bed you slept in doesn't exist, you get sent back to the world's spawn point!

63 Never try to carry too much when you're exploring underground. Use chests to create small temporary storage areas; otherwise, if you die before you make it back to your base, you'll end up losing everything!

64 If you're exploring underwater, you can place doors and fence posts to create "airlocks" that allow you to breathe without returning to the surface.

65 It's possible to fish in tiny amounts of water, even when you're underground. Keep a rod on you when exploring caves and it will be easy to keep your hunger down.

You can fish in any amount of water

66 You probably know you can skip nights in Minecraft by sleeping in a bed, but did you know you can also skip rainstorms the same way? You'll wake up to nothing but daylight, and the rain will be long gone!

67 You can build shortcuts through the Nether to travel long distances. Every step you take there is equivalent to eight in the Overworld so journey times are shortened, though it's a lot riskier!

Take shortcuts through the Nether – if you dare!

68 You can walk on lilypads while they're floating. They're a way to get out of the water for a bit, or to make bridges!

69 Boats are faster than walking, so if you're travelling or exploring a new area, sticking to water will allow you to cover more ground than clambering over uneven terrain.

Boats are faster than walking

70 Remember to pull up the carpet in igloos to see if they've generated a basement underneath. Only 50% of igloos have basements,

CONTINUED ON PAGE 54!

HAVE YOU FOUND THESE IN MINECRAFT?

Minecraft is full of weird and rare things to find. Some are put there for you, while others appear on their own. But if you want to get a sneak peek of what's out there, here's a list of things you might encounter – but only if you're lucky!

Horse Armour

Riding horses is a great way to cover long distances quickly, so when you find a good, strong horse you must look after it. That's why you need horse armour. You can find horse armour in chests, but only very rarely. There are three types of horse armour: iron, gold and diamond. Diamond is the strongest and rarest, and protects your horse against almost 50% of damage inflicted. Horse armour has infinite durability, so once you find it you don't ever have to repair it.

Armour protects your horse

Dragon Egg

To find a dragon egg, you have to kill the ender dragon. It takes a lot of work to find the ender dragon, so don't expect to kill it for a long time! When you do, a dragon egg appears on top of the exit portal to the Overworld. It's hard to collect, as it teleports away if you interact with it, but trick it into breaking by digging underneath it, placing a torch two blocks below it, then breaking the block between it and the torch to make it fall down.

It's hard to collect the dragon egg, but not impossible

The Nether Star

If you manage to summon and kill the wither, you can collect a Nether star. This is harder than defeating the ender dragon, so the Nether star is probably the rarest item in the game. Use them to create beacon blocks by crafting them with obsidian and glass.

Kill the wither to get a Nether star

Records (Music Discs)

There are 12 music discs in Minecraft, which you can collect and play in a jukebox. On the Console Edition, you can find them all in the tutorial world, but on other editions only two songs are generated naturally – Cat and 13 – both of which have a chance of appearing in around one in five dungeon chests. The others are only dropped if a skeleton accidentally kills a creeper. Watch out for disc 11, which is broken!

Music discs go in jukeboxes

Eat an enchanted golden apple for special effects

Enchanted Golden Apples

In the past, golden apples, which give you the absorption and regeneration effects, could be crafted by surrounding a normal apple with gold ingots, but that's no longer the case. In current versions of the game, they can only be found in desert temple chests, dungeon chests and abandoned minecart chests. Eating one gives you the Absorption IV, Regeneration II, Fire Resistance I and Resistance I effects, but you can also use one to add a coloured Mojang logo to a banner (by crafting it with dye and a banner).

Sponge

Sponges are almost impossible to get without resorting to Creative mode. If you're playing in Survival, the only place you can find them is inside ocean monuments, where occasionally rooms are full of them. It's also possible to collect a sponge by killing elder guardians, which spawn in ocean monuments. Wherever you get them from, they'll start life as a "wet sponge" and you'll have to dry them out in a furnace before you can use them.

Sponges in a monument

43

Multi-Villages

Due to the way villages spawn in Minecraft, it's possible (but rare!) for more than one to spawn so close to each other that they appear as one giant village. Every village contains a single well, so if you find a large settlement with more than one well it's because it's two on top of each other. There's no real benefit, it's just good fun to find larger villages! We've seen three and even four together before, so keep an eye out!

An igloo basement

Several villages together

Igloo Basement

Igloos are a relatively new addition to the game, so there's a chance you don't realise that half of all igloos also have a basement. If you collect the carpet inside an igloo, you might find a trapdoor, and if you head down the long access tunnel below it you'll arrive in a small cellar containing everything you need to try and turn a zombie villager back into a regular villager, including a golden apple and potion of weakness. It's also the easiest way to get a brewing stand – you don't even have to visit the Nether this way!

Ocean Strongholds

Most strongholds, which are large underground fortresses made out of stone, appear deep underground, but occasionally they can accidentally generate in the sea.

The way strongholds form means that if one appears underwater, only the End portal room generates, so if you come across one, it's worth marking down exactly where it is so you'll be able to access the End without having to fight your way through a mazelike stronghold!

A glitched ocean stronghold

Mooshrooms

Mooshrooms only appear in the mushroom island biome, and are very hard to find under any circumstances. Like regular cows, they can be "milked", but you get mushroom stew as well as milk.

You can convert mooshrooms back into regular cows using a pair of shears. This gives you five red mushrooms. If you kill a mooshroom, it only drops leather and beef like a normal cow.

Spider jockeys combine a skeleton with a spider

A mooshroom in its habitat

Chicken Jockey & Spider Jockey

All spiders have a 1% chance of spawning with a skeleton riding them. This combination is known as a spider jockey. The skeletons and spiders can be killed separately, but the combination makes them really quite dangerous to approach!

Chicken jockeys are chickens with baby zombie riders. Any baby zombie that spawns has a 5% chance of being on a chicken, plus there's a chance they can mount a chicken if they come into contact with one. Chicken jockeys move much faster than a regular chicken and don't take fall damage.

Charged Creeper

If a creeper is struck by lightning, it becomes a charged creeper. You can spot one by its blue aura. Charged creepers set off much bigger explosions than regular ones, with twice the range, though their countdown timers are the same. If you want to collect mob heads, lure a charged creeper near to a skeleton, zombie, wither skeleton or creeper and make sure it kills it in the explosion. You can collect one mob head per explosion!

A charged creeper

MINECRAFT'S BEST HIDDEN SECRETS

Minecraft's developers are keen to put little jokes and surprises in the game for people to find. Here are a few of the best hidden secrets that have been discovered over the years!

Steve Co. Supply Crate

The joke chest

You need a Steve Co. Supply Crate Key to open this. You can pick one up at the Minecraft store.

Not now   Go to store

April Fools' Day

The PC version has occasionally been updated with small jokes, especially for April Fools' Day.

In 2011, the developers added a "locked chest" to the game as a joke. For one week, anyone trying to open it would be told they had to buy a key from the Minecraft store. It was intended as a joke about paid-for downloads and mobile games – there wasn't actually anything to buy and the chest couldn't be opened!

In 2013, every player's skin was changed to a generic villager for 24 hours, while a post on the Minecraft blog explained the villagers (which had just been added to the game) had become sentient and taken over the servers.

There aren't jokes every year, but it's always worth firing up your copy of the game on 1st April!

> On 1st April, see if anything fun has happened!

Halloween Masks

On 31st October, any mob that can wear armour – zombies, skeletons, pigmen and wither skeletons – can spawn wearing pumpkins or Jack 'O' Lanterns on their heads. This has happened every year since 2012! It's possible to collect the blocks by killing the mobs with a sword carrying the looting enchantment; otherwise, they disappear when the mob dies.

In addition, the only splash text on the title screen on Halloween is "OOoooOOOoooo! Spooky!"

Mobs wearing pumpkins

The player can wear pumpkins, too

Christmas Presents

In 2012, 2013 and 2014, if you played Minecraft between 24 and 26 December all of the chests turned into giant presents. Small ones were red with a yellow bow, and big ones were green with a white bow. In 2014, the splash text also read "Merry X-Mas".

We don't know whether it will happen again – it didn't in 2015 – but it's always worth looking out for at Christmas!

Upside-Down Mobs

If you use a nametag to give a mob the name "Dinnerbone" or "Grumm" (with capital letters) it will be rendered upside down. You can also rename a spawn egg to spawn upside-down mobs. Dinnerbone and Grumm are two of Minecraft's developers and are responsible for adding this Easter egg into the game!

Multicoloured Sheep

If you use a nametag on a sheep to rename it "jeb_" (no capitals, with the underscore) its wool will cycle through every available colour. Shearing the sheep will only get you the original colour wool, however, so a white sheep still only drops white wool, regardless of what colour you see.

Again, you can rename a spawn egg in this way to make it spawn only multicoloured sheep.

Jeb is the lead creative designer for both Minecraft and Minecraft Pocket Edition. He's responsible for adding pistons, wolves, villages, strongholds and Nether fortresses to the game, plus other things!

"Grumm" or "Dinnerbone" nametags turn mobs upside down

Christmas chests

A pig named Dinnerbone

Dinnerbone

A sheep named jeb_ changes colours

jeb_

Does the broken record contain the face of herobrine?

The killer rabbit of Caerbannog

Toast, the unique rabbit skin

Toast

The killer bunny doesn't just spawn naturally

Broken Record

If you've ever found Disc 11 and tried to play it in a jukebox, you'll remember it as the broken record that plays a weird and distorted tune. But there's actually a secret behind the sounds it's making. If you run them through a spectrogram – a program that turns soundwaves into visible waves – you can see a picture of a Minecraft character's face. Some speculate this is the face of the mysterious ghost Minecrafter, Herobrine!

It's also possible to see the number "12418", which is a reference to Minecraft's soundtrack composer, C418 – the number "12" represents the letter "C" in the computer language of hexadecimal.

Killer Bunny

The killer bunny mob is a variant rabbit that's hostile to players, wolves and dogs. At present, it doesn't spawn naturally and can only be added using the "summon" console command. It's a reference to the "killer rabbit of Caerbannog" from the film *Monty Python and The Holy Grail*. The killer bunny doesn't despawn, even in peaceful mode, but won't attack the player (but will still attack wolves and dogs).

Toast the Rabbit

Another variant rabbit can be created by using a nametag to give a rabbit the name "Toast" (with the capital letter). Toast looks similar to other black and white rabbits, but has more black fur on its face. It was added by developer Ryan Holtz to commemorate the missing rabbit of Minecraft user xyZenTV.

Golden Tower

In the TU12-13 Console Edition, if you went to the top of the sandstone pyramid in the tutorial world you'd find a block of obsidian with four blocks of gold on top of it. This tower was initially created by Gavin Free from the Achievement Hunter online video series and has become a symbol of their "Let's Play Minecraft" series.

Stampylonghead's House

In the TU19 Console Edition tutorial world, there's an island in the north-east with an old version of Stampylonghead's house, along with his boat, the S.S. Stumpy.

Minceraft

There's a 0.01% chance that the title screen will read "Minceraft" not Minecraft. It was added by Notch, but nobody noticed for years! It was only found when he admitted there was something in the game that hadn't been spotted, prompting people to go looking.

Portal Reference

The achievement you get for crafting a cake is called "The Lie". This is a reference to the videogame Portal, which featured the slogan "The Cake is a Lie" in reference to the rewards promised to the main character's capturers.

Enchanting Symbols

The enchantment symbols can't be translated in any useful way, but they're actually taken from the "Standard Galactic Alphabet" invented by Tom Hall for the 1990s PC game, Commander Keen.

There's a tiny chance the title says "Minceraft"

Golden towers like this are an in-joke

The Cake is a Lie

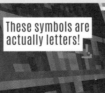

These symbols are actually letters!

THE BEST RECIPES

With tonnes of recipes at your fingertips, it can sometimes be hard to decide just what to craft. To help you, we've chosen some of our favourites for you to try out. Enjoy!

There's no end to the number of recipes Minecraft contains. You probably know the most common ones – how to make a boat, pickaxe, bucket, or even TNT – but what else is there that you might have missed? It's hard to figure out how to craft something if you don't know the ingredients, so to help you we've collected together the best recipes you might not know about.

Sea Lantern

Ingredients
- 5 x Prismarine crystals
- 4 x Prismarine shards

Sea lanterns can be found in ocean monuments, but break if mined, so you have to craft them. Get prismarine crystals by killing guardians or shattering existing sea lanterns, and prismarine shards by mining prismarine blocks.

Ender Chest

Ingredients
- 1 x Eye of ender
- 8 x Obsidian

Ender chests differ from normal chests in that every chest opens to the same storage area, so you can use them to access and transfer items across huge distances without needing to carry them. Obsidian can be mined with a diamond pickaxe and eyes of ender are created by crafting blaze powder with an ender pearl.

Redstone Lamp

Ingredients

- 4 x Redstone dust
- 1 x Glowstone block

Redstone lamps can be switched on and off with a redstone charge. Place a lever next to them to create a simple light switch. Redstone dust can be mined underground, and glowstone blocks can be crafted out of 4 x glowstone dust.

Rabbit Stew

Ingredients

- 1 x Cooked rabbit
- 1 x Baked potato
- 1 x Mushroom
- 1 x Carrot
- 1 x Bowl

Rabbit stew restores 10 hunger points, which is less than its ingredients restore separately, but the hunger is highly saturated and the ingredients take up less space.

Cookies

Ingredients

- 2 x Wheat
- 1 x Cocoa beans

This recipe crafts eight cookies. Each cookie restores one hunger point (half an icon). Cookies only restore a small amount of hunger points, so nothing is wasted!

Cake

Ingredients

- 3 x Milk
- 1 x Egg
- 2 x Sugar
- 3 x Wheat

Cake is a great way to store food because you can place it in block form then eat it. Eating a cake restores a great deal of hunger and makes use of some otherwise limited items.

Hay Bales

Ingredients

- 9 x Wheat

Hay bales are the only food items you can craft that other mobs eat, as horses, mules and donkeys can feed on them to restore health. You can also use hay bales to store wheat – they can be crafted back into wheat on a crafting table.

Armour Stand

Ingredients
- 1 x Stone slab
- 6 x Sticks

You can use an armour stand to display armour, clothing, and other wearable items like mob heads and pumpkins. They also make good scarecrows! There's no practical use for armour stands that couldn't be accomplished by a chest, but they make for good decoration!

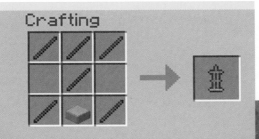

Bookshelves

Ingredients
- 6 x Wood planks
- 3 x Books

Bookshelves break if you mine them, but you can easily craft them by combining books and wood. They can be used as decoration or to store books, but their best use is to power up an enchantment table so that it can imbue items with higher level enchantments.

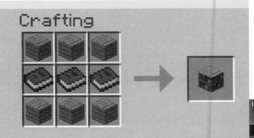

Fence Gates

Ingredients
- 2 x Wood planks
- 4 x Sticks

Fence gates can be opened and closed like doors, and like fences they can't be jumped over. The colour of a fence gate depends on the type of wood planks you use to craft it. Like doors, it's also possible to then control them by using redstone power.

Anvil

Ingredients
- 3 x Blocks of iron
- 4 x Iron ingots

Anvils can be used to rename and repair enchanted items without losing the enchantments, and are affected by gravity, so you can use them in traps! It takes 31 iron ingots in total to craft an anvil – 9 for each of 3 blocks of iron, plus 4 extra for its base.

Brewing Stand

Ingredients

- 1 x Blaze rod
- 3 x Cobblestone

A brewing stand allows you to filter ingredients into water bottles to create up to three potions at once. They can be generated in End cities and igloo basements, though for them to be of any use you must also collect blaze powder (crafted from blaze rods) by visiting the Nether.

End Rod

Ingredients

- 1 x Popped chorus fruit
- 1 x Blaze rod

These weird light sources are found only in the End, and this recipe will create four of them. To craft them, you need a blaze rod and a popped chorus fruit. To pop a chorus fruit, collect one from a chorus tree then bake it in a furnace.

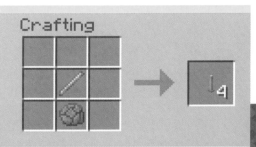

End Crystal

Ingredients

- 1 x Eye of ender
- 1 x Ghast tear
- 7 x Glass blocks

End crystals are found in the End, where they heal the ender dragon. They can also summon a new ender dragon if you place them on the exit portal in the End after killing the first dragon. They can only sit on obsidian or bedrock blocks.

Shield

Ingredients

- 6 x Wood planks
- 1 x Iron ingot

Shields are a defensive item introduced in Minecraft 1.9 early in 2016. They can block attacks and bounce arrows fired at you. It's also possible to change their appearance by crafting them with a banner – the shield will take on the banner's patterns and colours.

101 WAYS TO BE A MINECRAFT EXPERT PART 3

MINING

Mining underwater is slow!

71 Don't try and mine when the top half of your body is underwater unless you have the Aqua Affinity enchantment; otherwise, blocks take five times as long to break (when you're standing on something) and 25 times as long (when you're not!).

72 Gold ore is normally found deep underground, but it can appear near the surface in mesa biomes, as can abandoned mines, but only in Pocket Edition at the moment. There's a chance this will happen in other editions of the game in the future!

Find gold ore near the surface in mesas

Silverfish hide in monster eggs

73 Diamond ore veins can generate diagonally, so break all of the blocks around any piece of ore you find to make sure you don't miss this valuable block.

Diamond generates in diagonal veins

74 If you're in extreme hills, a stronghold or an igloo basement, watch out for monster egg blocks. They look normal, but break a little slower than you'd expect and then release silverfish when they're finally destroyed.

75 When you're exploring, always place torches on the left-hand side of a wall so that you can tell where you've been and where you haven't. That way, you can always find your way back to the surface by keeping the torches on your right.

76 If you encounter a dead end while exploring, you might also want to block it off with a bar of cobblestone so that you don't accidentally go down there again. Place a torch on the front so that if you ever encounter it from the other side, you know where you blocked it off from.

77 It's quicker to discover diamonds in caves than it is to mine for them. They usually appear near underground lava lakes, so follow the edges of those and you should find diamonds quite easily.

54

BLOCKS

78 Snow and ice blocks can be melted by a heat source, but won't get melted by sunlight alone. Packed ice doesn't even melt near heat, but can't be crafted, only collected from an ice spike with a silk touch pickaxe.

Igloos are made of packed snow

79 You can reuse a wet sponge over and over again by drying it out in a furnace. If there's an empty bucket in the fuel slot, then drying out a sponge will fill it with water; otherwise, the water simply disappears.

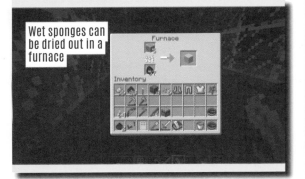
Wet sponges can be dried out in a furnace

80 You probably know you can activate iron and snow golems by putting a pumpkin on top of them, but did you know you that Jack 'O'Lanterns work just as well? It won't make the golem look any different, though!

81 One coal block (crafted from nine coal) burns in a furnace for as long as 10 coal pieces, so if you craft one instead of using just coal, you essentially get a bonus piece for your trouble!

82 If there's a drop within six blocks of a water source block, the water itself will automatically flow towards it; otherwise, it just spreads out evenly in every direction.

Water flows towards holes

83 If you need to blow up some TNT, don't just set it on fire with a flint and steel then run. Instead, use redstone dust to create a "fuse" and activate it from a safe distance with a redstone charge.

84 You can craft glowstone without ever visiting the Nether by collecting glowstone dust dropped by witches. It's ideal if you're trying to avoid a particularly difficult fight!

85 Soul sand makes mobs (and players) stick to it, so you can trap them by surrounding soul sand with slabs that let them in easily, but stop them stepping out.

SECRETS

86 Usually, you can't jump over walls and fences, but place a piece of carpet on top and it suddenly becomes possible. You can leave it there to create a stile that won't let mobs in and out (other than rabbits, which can jump high enough to use it).

Place carpet on walls to jump over them easily

87 Using a nametag on a mob prevents it from despawning, although it's still possible for it to die. If the mob is hostile, it will also disappear if you set the difficulty to peaceful.

88 You can place trapped chests next to regular ones without a gap, which allows you to pack them more closely together. They don't have to set off a trap!

89 Soul sand will suffocate silverfish and endermites,

Trapped chests sit fine against normal chests

causing them to die. You can use this knowledge to trap silverfish in strongholds.

90 Placing carpet or layers of snow on soul sand will completely negate its effects, allowing you – and other mobs – to walk and jump on it normally.

91 The storage area inside ender chests is unique to each player, so you can use them to completely hide items from other players in multiplayer worlds. Even destroying the chest won't destroy your stuff – you just have to build a new one.

92 You can submerge yourself in water to largely escape the effects of TNT or a creeper explosion – they'll barely touch you then!

Use ender chests to hide items

93 End gateways only generate when you kill an ender dragon (a challenge in itself). You can use them to teleport around the End by throwing ender pearls into them. Every ender dragon you kill generates a new End gateway, and when you travel through one it generates an exit gateway so you can get back.

An End gateway

TIPS & TRICKS

94 Make a map of your base area and place it on the wall in an item frame so that any visitors to your world can easily see what's around them. The location of the map is marked by a green blob.

95 Craft together nine slimeballs to make a slime block, which slows down anything that walks on it and can bounce you high in the air if you jump down on it from a great height – without damaging you!

Slime blocks will break your fall

96 You don't have to put coal in furnaces. Almost anything wooden can burn, including saplings, so it's a useful way of getting rid of junk and hanging onto valuable coal.

97 If you want to collect lots of snow, build a snow golem in a small pit or dark room (make sure it doesn't get too hot!) and it will generate a layer of snow as it wanders around, which you can easily harvest.

Iron bars can create a grate

98 Four iron bars in a square creates an off-centre gap that players can drop through, but water and lava can't. You can use this to create secret gates hidden from other players.

99 When you're in the Nether, use Nether bricks (which you can craft out of Netherrack) to build shelters. Ghast fireballs can't destroy Nether bricks, so you should be safe inside one.

Ghast fireballs won't break Nether bricks

100 Incinerators are useful for getting rid of blocks, but lava and fire can damage both you and your base. If you want to quickly destroy unwanted items, use a piece of cactus instead.

101 Rather than destroy a monster spawner, dig a huge pit beneath it so any new mobs that spawn instantly fall to their death. You'll quickly rack up experience and item drops without a lot of work.

Use monster spawners to farm mobs

ARE YOU A MINECRAFT EXPERT?

Reckon you know Minecraft like the back of your hand? Then take our quiz and find out if you're a crafting expert! You'll find the answers on page 63!

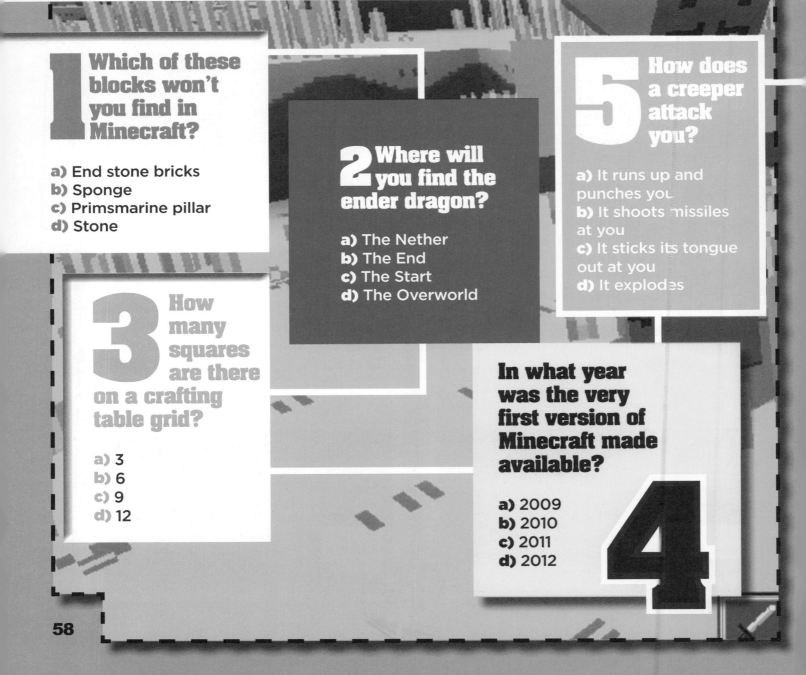

1 Which of these blocks won't you find in Minecraft?

a) End stone bricks
b) Sponge
c) Primsmarine pillar
d) Stone

2 Where will you find the ender dragon?

a) The Nether
b) The End
c) The Start
d) The Overworld

5 How does a creeper attack you?

a) It runs up and punches you
b) It shoots missiles at you
c) It sticks its tongue out at you
d) It explodes

3 How many squares are there on a crafting table grid?

a) 3
b) 6
c) 9
d) 12

4 In what year was the very first version of Minecraft made available?

a) 2009
b) 2010
c) 2011
d) 2012

6 What do you need to craft an arrow?

a) String + Flint + Stick
b) Flint + Stick + Feather
c) Feather + Stick + String
d) String + Flint

7 YouTuber Joseph Garrett is best known by what name?

a) Sqaishey Quack
b) Squid
c) Stampy
d) The Diamond Minecart

8 If you want to lure an ocelot, what food type should you use?

a) Raw fish
b) Carrots
c) Golden carrots
d) Potatoes

9 Which of these games consoles was the LAST to have Minecraft released for it?

a) The PSP
b) The Xbox One
c) The Nintendo WiiU
d) The PlayStation 4

10 Here's a tricky one! What was the original name of Minecraft?

a) Mineworld
b) The Mining Game
c) Cave Game
d) Craftworld

11 What weather makes it easier to catch fish?

a) Makes no difference
b) Rain
c) Sunshine
d) Cloud

12 Who created Minecraft in the first place?

a) Stampy
b) Jeb
c) Alex
d) Notch

13 If lightning strikes within four blocks of a pig, what will appear?

a) Some meat
b) A zombie pigman
c) Gold nuggets
d) Rotten flesh

14 Which of these is a type of golem you can find in Minecraft?

a) A fire golem
b) A steel golem
c) A snow golem
d) A zombie golem

15 How many episodes were released as part of Minecraft: Story Mode?

a) 4
b) 5
c) 6
d) 7

18

By default, what colour is Alex's top?

a) Brown
b) Orange
c) Green
d) Blue

19 Which of these will NOT spawn in the Nether?

a) Wither skeleton
b) Ghast
c) Guardian
d) Blaze

17 Which of these mobs is tameable?

a) Blaze
b) Enderman
c) Silverfish
d) Wolf

20 You've got to the last question! Which of these biomes is the warmest?

a) Jungle
b) Beach
c) Taiga
d) Savanna

16 What item does a spider drop?

a) Wool
b) String
c) Bones
d) Carrots